D1639437

LOW-CALORIE COOKBOOK

Editor:
Valerie Ferguson

LORENZ BOOKS

Contents

Introduction

Eating a low-calorie diet that is healthy, delicious and visually appealing has never been easier. With the vast range of excellent food products available in the shops, and our clearer understanding of the calorific value of the various food groups (fats, carbohydrates, etc) and how the body uses them, it is no longer difficult to put together truly tasty and interesting meals that will not pile on the pounds.

This book offers a varied selection of recipes for soups, starters, fish, seafood, poultry, meat and vegetarian dishes, plus desserts with modest calorie counts that will amaze you. Try Cream of Grilled Pepper Soup. Enjoy Poached Salmon with Citrus Fruits, Skewered Lamb with Red Onion Salsa or Rice Noodles with Vegetable Chilli Sauce. Indulge in scrumptious Strawberry Gâteau. You will find it hard to believe that all of these are low-calorie dishes.

Nutritional Notes are provided for each recipe, giving the calorie count per serving – soups and starters generally average 170 calories, main courses 210–310 calories and desserts 200 calories. Enjoy combining our recipes as part of your calorie-controlled diet.

4

Planning a Low-calorie Diet

Everyone needs the calories obtained from food as these provide the energy required to go about daily life. However, some people take in too many calories by eating too much or the wrong kind of food and may then put on excess weight.

The average daily requirement for women is 1,940 calories, and 2,550 calories for men. Most women can lose up to 4 lbs a month on a healthy diet of 1,200– 1,500 calories (1,500–1,750 for men) a day.

How to Cut Down

The Calorie Content of Food table shows at a glance which foods are high in calories and which are not; use this as a guide. It is clear from the table that fats (such as oil and butter) and foods containing more than a little of these are the worst culprits, and foods high in carbohydrates (such as sugar) are also far from blameless. In fact, fats supply about 9 calories per gram, while carbohydrates provide about 4 calories per gram.

No matter how careful you are, you can be caught out by pre-prepared and packaged foods, such as biscuits, pastries and chocolates, which, as well as being high in sugar, can contain large amounts of "hidden" fat, which boosts their calorific value considerably. Nowadays such foods come with a breakdown of their contents, including calories, on the label and you will find that you soon become accustomed to checking this and avoiding, or at least limiting, your consumption of them.

Above: Vegetables are vital ingredients for healthy, low-calorie meals.

Keep Eating a Balanced Diet

Current recommendations for a nutritionally balanced diet are to include a moderate amount of red meat, poultry and fish. Starchy foods (rice, pasta and bread) should provide 50 per cent of total calorie intake. At least five portions of fresh fruit and vegetables should be eaten daily. For example, one apple is a portion.

The red meats – lamb, beef and pork – are the highest in fat, and hence in calories, so it is advisable to choose chicken and turkey more often. Select lean cuts and remove the skin and any visible fat before cooking. Avoid sausages, pâtés, and pies which are usually laden with calories. Fish, particularly white fish and shellfish, are generally lower in calories than meat and are highly nutritious, so are a good choice for calorie-watchers.

Fresh vegetables and fruit, with the exception of high-fat avocados, are

Above: Fruit is delicious and healthy.

naturally low in calories. Nuts should be eaten in small amounts as they are high in calories. Alcohol is also high in calories and should be taken sparingly.

Cooking Methods

Whenever possible, grill, griddle, poach, steam or bake foods. If you have to fry, use as little fat as possible. Make sauces and stews by first cooking the onions and garlic in a small quantity of stock.

Labelling

Read labels carefully when choosing food. If a product claims to be low in calories, it should provide no more than 40 calories per 100 grams or 100 ml. A "reduced-calorie" product should provide no more than 75 per cent of the calories found in the standard product..

The Calorie Content of Food

This chart shows the energy content (measured in calories) of 25 g/1 oz of different foods.

Breads, cereals, biscuits & preserves / Energy

Bread, white	59 Kcals/251 kJ
Bread, wholemeal (whole-wheat)	54 Kcals/228 kJ
Rice, white, uncooked	90 Kcals/384 kJ
Pasta, white, uncooked	86 Kcals/364 kJ
Cake, fruit, plain, store-bought	89 Kcals/372 kJ
Jam	65 Kcals/273 kJ
Chocolate, plain	127 Kcals/534 kJ

Eggs & oils

Egg, boiled (half an egg)	37 Kcals/153 kJ
Egg, white	9 Kcals/38 kJ
Egg, yolk	85 Kcals/351 kJ
Oil, sunflower	225 Kcals/924 kJ
Oil, olive	225 Kcals/924 kJ

Poultry, meat & meat products

Chicken, roast, meat & skin	54 Kcals/226 kJ
Chicken, roast, meat only	37 Kcals/155 kJ
Turkey, roast, meat & skin	43 Kcals/179 kJ
Turkey, roast, meat only	35 Kcals/148 kJ
Bacon, back, grilled, fat trimmed	53 Kcals/223 kJ
Beef, roast, topside, lean	39 Kcals/165 kJ
Lamb, loin chop, grilled, lean	62 Kcals/260 kJ
Lamb, leg, roast, lean	53 Kcals/220 kJ
Pork, loin chop, grilled, lean	46 Kcals/193 kJ
Liver pâté	87 Kcals/359 kJ
Pork pie, individual	94 Kcals/391 kJ

Fish

Cod, raw	20 Kcals/84 kJ
Cod, fried in batter	61 Kcals/255 kJ
Prawns (shrimp), cooked, no shell	25 Kcals/105 kJ
Salmon, canned	38 Kcals/161 kJ
Salmon, grilled	54 Kcals/224 kJ
Trout, grilled	34 Kcals/141 kJ
Tuna, raw	34 Kcals/141 kJ
Tuna, canned in brine	25 Kcals/106 kJ

Vegetables

Broccoli, boiled	6 Kcals/25 kJ
Brussels sprouts, boiled	9 Kcals/37 kJ
Cauliflower, boiled	7 Kcals/29 kJ
Celery, raw	2 Kcals/8 kJ
Courgettes (zucchini), boiled	5 Kcals/20 kJ
Mushrooms, raw	3 Kcals/12 kJ
Leeks, boiled	5 Kcals/22 kJ
Peas, boiled	17 Kcals/73 kJ
Peppers, raw	4 Kcals/16 kJ
Potatoes, new, boiled	19 Kcals/78 kJ
Chips (French fries), oven baked	39 Kcals/166 kJ
Chips, fried, retail	59 Kcals/246 kJ
Tomatoes, raw	4 Kcals/18 kJ

Fruit & nuts

Apple	11 Kcals/45 kJ
Avocado	48 Kcals/196 kJ
Banana	24 Kcals/101 kJ
Dried mixed fruit	67 Kcals/281 kJ
Orange	9 Kcals/39 kJ
Peach	8 Kcals/35 kJ
Strawberries	7 Kcals/28 kJ
Almonds	153 Kcals/633 kJ
Cashews, roasted	153 Kcals/633 kJ
Coconut, desiccated	151 Kcals/623 kJ
Peanuts, roasted	150 Kcals/623 kJ
Sesame seeds	148 Kcals/618 kJ

Dairy produce

Cream, double (heavy)	112 Kcals/462 kJ
Cream, single (light)	49 Kcals/204 kJ
Milk, whole	16 Kcals/69 kJ
Milk, semi-skimmed (low-fat)	11 Kcals/49 kJ
Milk, skimmed (skim)	8 Kcals/35 kJ
Margarine	185 Kcals/760 kJ
Butter	184 Kcals/758 kJ
Low-fat spread (40%)	98 Kcals/401 kJ
Very low-fat spread (25%)	68 Kcals/282 kJ
Crème fraîche	78 Kcals/324 kJ
Crème fraîche, low fat	42 Kcals/173 kJ
Fromage frais	28 Kcals/117 kJ
Fromage frais, very low fat	15 Kcals/62 kJ
Cheese, Cheddar	103 Kcals/427 kJ
Cheese, Cheddar, reduced fat	65 Kcals/273 kJ
Cheese, Edam	83 Kcals/346 kJ
Yogurt, plain, low fat	13 Kcals/54 kJ
Greek yogurt (plain, strained)	29 Kcals/119 kJ

Low-calorie Ingredients & Substitutes

To help with your calorie-controlled diet, look out for the many lower fat and lower sugar or "diet" versions of standard foods now available.

Dairy Produce

Milk Choose semi-skimmed (low-fat) (1.5–1.8 per cent fat) or skimmed (skim) (0.3 per cent fat) milk.

Yogurt Low-fat (about 1 per cent fat) and "diet" (0.3 per cent fat) natural yogurts are an excellent substitute for cream.

Crème fraîche Delicious served with desserts and successful in cooking, the half-fat version contains about 15 per cent fat.

Fromage frais A fresh-tasting soft cheese, available as virtually fat-free (0.4 per cent fat). Useful as an accompaniment for desserts and for filling and topping cakes.

Cottage cheese A low-fat soft cheese, which is also available in a half-fat version.

Half fat hard cheese Several kinds of hard cheese are now obtainable in half-fat form, including Cheddar and Red Leicester (both about 14 per cent fat).

Above: Low-fat yogurt and cheeses are widely available in supermarkets.

Spreads

For spreading on bread, try reduced-fat butter or a low-fat spread made with a high proportion of buttermilk or with sunflower or olive oil, all of which contain about 40 per cent fat. There are also very low-fat spreads that contain 20–30 per cent fat. None of these reduced-fat spreads is suitable for baking.

Sweeteners

Sugar and honey As these are both high in calories, they should be used sparingly. Dark sugar and honey have more flavour so you can usually get away with using less.

Artificial sweeteners Available in liquid, granulated and "tablet" form, these are a useful alternative to sugar for sweetening recipes and drinks. Most contain about one-tenth the calories of sugar.

Fruit spreads and juices Use concentrated, unsweetened fruit spreads and juices sparingly as sweeteners for all kinds of desserts.

Tomato & Basil-flower Soup

A pretty, fresh-tasting chilled soup with a low calorie count.

Serves 4

INGREDIENTS
1 onion, chopped
1 garlic clove, crushed
15 ml/1 tbsp olive oil
600 ml/1 pint/2½ cups vegetable stock
900 g/2 lb tomatoes, roughly chopped
20 basil leaves, plus extra to garnish
few drops of elderflower or balsamic vinegar
juice of ½ lemon
150 ml/¼ pint/⅔ cup plain low-fat yogurt
sugar and salt, to taste
30 ml/2 tbsp plain low-fat yogurt and
    10 ml/2 tsp basil flowers, to garnish

1 Fry the onion and garlic in the oil for 2–3 minutes until soft. Add 300 ml/ ½ pint/1¼ cups of the stock and the tomatoes. Bring to the boil, lower the heat and simmer for 15 minutes.

2 Allow to cool slightly, then process in a blender or food processor. Strain. Add the remaining stock, half the basil leaves, the vinegar, lemon juice and yogurt to the puréed tomatoes. Season with sugar and salt to taste. Process until smooth. Chill.

3 Just before serving, finely shred the remaining basil leaves and add to the soup. Pour into individual bowls. Garnish with yogurt topped with a few small basil leaves and flowers and serve.

Nutritional Notes	
Energy	97 Kcals/403 kJ
Fat, total	3.8 g
Saturated fat	0.8 g
Cholesterol	1.5 mg

Spicy Tomato & Lentil Soup

This warming soup is flavoured with a hint of fresh ginger and cumin.

Serves 4

INGREDIENTS
15 ml/1 tbsp sunflower oil
1 onion, finely chopped
1–2 garlic cloves, crushed
2.5 cm/1 in piece fresh root ginger, peeled
  and finely chopped
5 ml/1 tsp cumin seed, crushed
450 g/1 lb ripe tomatoes, peeled, seeded and
  chopped
115 g/4 oz/½ cup split red lentils
1.2 litres/2 pints/5 cups vegetable or chicken
  stock
15 ml/1 tbsp tomato purée (paste)
salt and freshly ground black pepper
low-fat plain yogurt and chopped fresh
  parsley, to garnish (optional)

1 Heat the oil and cook the onion gently for about 5 minutes until softened. Add the garlic, ginger, cumin, tomatoes and lentils. Cook over a low heat for a further 3–4 minutes.

2 Stir in the stock and tomato purée. Bring to the boil, and simmer gently for about 30 minutes until the lentils are soft. Season to taste.

3 Purée the soup in a blender or food processor. Reheat, then serve garnished with a little yogurt and parsley, if liked.

Nutritional Notes	
Energy	151 Kcals/628 kJ
Fat, total	3.5 g
Saturated fat	0.5 g
Cholesterol	0 mg

Cream of Grilled Pepper Soup

This is a creamy but light, nutritious and colourful soup.

Serves 4

INGREDIENTS
3 large red (bell) peppers, halved and seeded
1 large yellow (bell) pepper, halved and
    seeded
15 ml/1 tbsp olive oil
1 small shallot, chopped
600 ml/1 pint/2½ cups vegetable stock
2 garlic cloves, crushed
1.5 ml/¼ tsp saffron strands
150 ml/¼ pint/⅔ cup single (light) cream
475 ml/16 fl oz/2 cups water
salt and freshly ground black pepper
fresh chervil or flat leaf parsley sprigs, to
    garnish and Melba toast, to serve

1 Grill (broil) the peppers until
blackened then place them in a plastic
bagand leave to cool. Peel, then reserve
one quarter each of a red and yellow
pepper and roughly chop the remainder.

2 Heat the oil and sauté the shallot
until soft. Add the stock, garlic, saffron
and chopped peppers. Bring to the boil
and simmer for 15 minutes. Cool for
10 minutes, then process in a blender
or food processor until smooth.

3 Return the soup to a clean pan.
Mix together the cream and water and
add to the soup with seasoning.
Reheat gently. Pour the soup into
bowls and garnish with thin strips of
the reserved peppers and herb sprigs.
Serve with Melba toast.

Nutritional Notes	
Energy	153 Kcals/636 kJ
Fat, total	10.5 g
Saturated fat	4.9 g
Cholesterol	20.6 mg

Farmhouse Soup

Root vegetables form the base of this chunky, minestrone-style soup.

Serves 4

INGREDIENTS

15 ml/1 tbsp olive oil
1 onion, roughly chopped
3 carrots, cut into chunks
150–175 g/5–6 oz turnips, cut into chunks
about 150 g/5 oz swede, cut into chunks
400 g/14 oz can chopped tomatoes
15 ml/1 tbsp tomato purée (paste)
5 ml/1 tsp dried mixed herbs
5 ml/1 tsp dried oregano
50 g/2 oz/½ cup dried (bell) peppers, washed
  and thinly sliced (optional)
1.5 litres/2½ pints/6¼ cups vegetable stock
  or water
50 g/2 oz/½ cup dried small macaroni
200 g/7 oz canned red kidney beans, rinsed
  and drained
30 ml/2 tbsp chopped fresh flat leaf parsley
salt and freshly ground black pepper
grated Parmesan cheese, to serve (optional)

1 Heat the oil and cook the onion for 5 minutes until softened. Add the next eight ingredients. Season to taste. Add the stock or water and bring to the boil. Cover and simmer for 30 minutes, stirring occasionally.

2 Add the pasta and bring to the boil, stirring. Simmer, uncovered, until the pasta is *al dente*.

3 Stir in the beans. Heat through for 2–3 minutes, then remove from the heat and add the parsley. Serve with grated Parmesan handed separately, if liked.

Nutritional Notes	
Energy	182 Kcals/756 kJ
Fat, total	3.8 g
Saturated fat	0.5 g
Cholesterol	0 mg

Chicken & Mushroom Terrine

Proof that a terrine can be mouthwatering without being calorie-loaded.

Serves 4

INGREDIENTS
2 shallots, chopped
175 g/6 oz/2 cups mushrooms, chopped
45 ml/3 tbsp chicken stock
2 skinless chicken breasts, chopped
1 egg white
30 ml/2 tbsp wholewheat breadcrumbs
30 ml/2 tbsp chopped fresh parsley
30 ml/2 tbsp chopped fresh sage
salt and freshly ground black pepper

1 Preheat the oven to 180°C/350°F/
Gas 4. Place the shallots, mushrooms
and stock in a pan and cook gently,
stirring occasionally, until the
vegetables have softened and the stock
has evaporated.

2 Place in a food processor with the
chopped chicken breasts, egg white,
breadcrumbs and seasoning and chop
coarsely. Add the herbs. Spoon into a
greased 900 ml/1½ pint/3¾ cup loaf
tin and smooth the surface.

3 Cover the tin with foil and bake for
35–40 minutes until the juices are no
longer pink. Place a weight on top,
leave to cool, then chill. Serve the
terrine sliced.

Nutritional Notes	
Energy	140 Kcals/582 kJ
Fat, total	2.9 g
Saturated fat	0.7 g
Cholesterol	61.0 mg

Guacamole with Crudités

This spicy dip is made using peas instead of the traditional avocados.

Serves 4–6

INGREDIENTS
350 g/12 oz/3 cups frozen peas, defrosted
1 garlic clove, crushed
2 spring onions(scallions), chopped
5 ml/1 tsp finely grated rind and juice of 1
    lime
2.5 ml/½ tsp ground cumin
dash of Tabasco sauce
15 ml/1 tbsp reduced-calorie mayonnaise
30 ml/2 tbsp chopped fresh coriander (cilantro)
1 dessert apple, cored and sliced
1 pear, peeled, cored and sliced
15 ml/1 tbsp lemon or lime juice
6 baby carrots
2 celery sticks, halved lengthways and cut
    into sticks
6 baby sweetcorn (baby corn)
salt and freshly ground black pepper
pinch of paprika and lime slices, to garnish

1 Put the first seven ingredients and seasoning into a food processor or a blender and process until smooth.

2 Add the coriander and process for a few more seconds. Spoon into a serving bowl, cover and chill for 30 minutes, to let the flavours develop.

3 Dip the apple and pear slices into the lemon or lime juice. Arrange with the carrots, celery and baby sweetcorn on a platter. Sprinkle the paprika over the guacamole, garnish with lime and serve with the crudités.

Nutritional Notes	
Energy	110 Kcals/460 kJ
Fat, total	2.29 g
Saturated fat	0.49 g
Cholesterol	30.0 mg

Vegetables Provençale

The flavours of the Mediterranean are created in this delicious vegetable dish, which makes an ideal low-calorie starter.

Serves 6

INGREDIENTS
1 onion, sliced
2 leeks, sliced
2 garlic cloves, crushed
1 red (bell) pepper, seeded and sliced
1 green (bell) pepper, seeded and sliced
1 yellow (bell) pepper, seeded and sliced
350 g/12 oz/2½ cups courgettes (zucchini), sliced
225 g/8 oz/3 cups mushrooms, sliced
400 g/14 oz can chopped tomatoes
30 ml/2 tbsp ruby port
30 ml/2 tbsp tomato purée (paste)
15 ml/1 tbsp tomato ketchup
400 g/14 oz can chickpeas
115 g/4 oz/1 cup pitted black olives
45 ml/3 tbsp chopped fresh mixed herbs, plus extra to garnish

2 Drain the chickpeas, rinse in cold water, drain again, then add to the pan. Stir well.

3 Cover, bring to the boil and simmer gently for 20–30 minutes until the vegetables are tender but not overcooked, stirring occasionally.

1 Put the onion, leeks, garlic, peppers, courgettes and mushrooms into a large pan. Add the tomatoes, port, tomato purée and tomato ketchup and mix thoroughly.

Nutritional Notes	
Energy	155 Kcals/654 kJ
Fat, total	4.56 g
Saturated fat	0.67 g
Cholesterol	0 mg

4 Remove the lid from the pan and increase the heat slightly for the last 10 minutes of the cooking time to thicken the sauce if liked.

5 Stir in the olives, chopped herbs and season with salt and pepper to taste. Serve hot or cold, garnished with chopped mixed herbs.

Monkfish Kebabs with Lemon & Thyme

These delicate, fresh flavourings are a perfect complement to monkfish.

Serves 4

INGREDIENTS
675 g/1½ lb monkfish fillet
15 ml/1 tbsp olive oil
1 garlic clove, crushed
finely grated rind and juice of 1 lemon
30 ml/2 tbsp chopped fresh thyme
8 lemon wedges
salt and freshly ground black pepper
green salad and crusty bread, to serve

1 Cut the fish into even-size pieces and place in a bowl. Add the oil, garlic, lemon rind and juice, thyme, and seasoning, then stir well to coat the fish evenly.

2 Preheat the grill (broiler) or prepare a barbecue. Thread the fish pieces on to four metal skewers and secure with lemon wedges at each end.

3 Cook the kebabs under the grill, or on the barbecue, for 7–8 minutes or until just cooked through, turning once. Serve with salad and bread.

Nutritional Notes	
Energy	136 Kcals/565 kJ
Fat, total	3.4 g
Saturated fat	0.5 g
Cholesterol	23.6 mg

Italian Fish Stew

A richly flavoured main course dish that is surprisingly low in calories.

Serves 4

INGREDIENTS
10 ml/2 tsp olive oil
1 medium red onion, finely chopped
1 garlic clove, crushed
1 small fennel bulb, sliced
400 g/14 oz can chopped tomatoes
10 ml/2 tsp fennel seeds
175 ml/6 fl oz/¾ cup fish stock
450 g/1 lb cod or haddock fillet, cut into
    chunks
15 g/½ oz/4 tbsp chopped fresh basil
4 lemon slices
salt and freshly ground black pepper

1 Heat the olive oil in a large pan
and fry the onion, garlic and sliced
fennel gently until they are softened
but not browned.

2 Add the tomatoes, fennel seeds and
fish stock and bring to the boil. Add
the diced fish, basil, lemon slices, salt
and pepper.

3 Cover and simmer very gently for
6–8 minutes until the fish is just
cooked through. Serve hot.

VARIATION: Almost any type of
white fish can be used in place of
the cod or haddock.

Nutritional Notes	
Energy	127 Kcals/528 kJ
Fat, total	2.6 g
Saturated fat	0.4 g
Cholesterol	43.8 mg

Whole Sea Bass
en Papillote

This way of cooking a whole fish enclosed in a paper parcel keeps it moist and retains the maximum flavour.

Serves 4

INGREDIENTS

1.5 kg/3–3½ lb fresh whole sea bass, cleaned, scaled and head removed
5 fresh mint sprigs
½ lemon, sliced
2 shallots, finely sliced
2 fresh plum tomatoes, sliced
15 ml/1 tbsp olive oil
salt and freshly ground black pepper
steamed broccoli, to serve

2 Season the fish inside and out with salt and pepper.

3 Tuck the fresh mint sprigs and lemon, shallots and tomato slices inside the fish and drizzle the olive oil over its back.

1 Preheat the oven to 180°C/350°F/ Gas 4. Wash and dry the sea bass and place on a double piece of nonstick baking parchment large enough to wrap the fish comfortably and loosely.

4 Fold the paper over the fish and double fold the three open edges for a tight seal. Place the fish on a baking sheet and bake for 40–50 minutes until cooked through.

5 Cut the package open with scissors and serve the fish immediately, accompanied by steamed broccoli.

Nutritional Notes	
Energy	301 Kcals/1252 kJ
Fat, total	15.3 g
Saturated fat	7.63 g
Cholesterol	163 mg

COOK'S TIP: Sea bass is also known as sea wolf, sea perch or sea dace and has delicate pink flesh and a light, sweet smell. Large fish are ideal for stuffing, as here, and small fish can be grilled or barbecued.

21

Monkfish & Scallop Skewers

Lemon grass imbues the seafood with a subtle citrus taste.

Serves 4

INGREDIENTS
8 lemon grass stalks
30 ml/2 tbsp lemon juice
15 ml/1 tbsp olive oil
15 ml/1 tbsp finely chopped fresh coriander
   (cilantro)
2.5 ml/½ tsp salt
large pinch of ground black pepper
450 g/1 lb monkfish fillet, cut into 16 chunks
12 large scallops, halved crossways
fresh coriander leaves, to garnish
rice, to serve

1 Remove the outer leaves from the lemon grass. Chop the tender parts of the lemon grass leaves finely and place in a bowl. Stir in the lemon juice, oil, chopped coriander, salt and pepper.

2 Thread the fish chunks and scallop halves alternately on the eight lemon grass stalks. Arrange the skewers of fish and shellfish in a shallow dish and pour over the lemon mixture.

3 Cover and leave to marinate for 1 hour, turning occasionally. Transfer the skewers to a heatproof dish or bamboo steamer, cover and steam over boiling water for 10 minutes until just cooked. Garnish with coriander and serve with rice and the cooking juice poured over.

Nutritional Notes	
Energy	158 Kcals/657 kJ
Fat, total	3.9 g
Saturated fat	0.7 g
Cholesterol	39.2 mg

Caribbean Fish Steaks

Serves 4

INGREDIENTS

15 ml/1 tbsp oil
6 shallots, finely chopped
1 garlic clove, crushed
1 fresh green chilli, seeded and finely
   chopped
400 g/14 oz can chopped tomatoes
2 bay leaves
1.5 ml/¼ tsp cayenne pepper
5 ml/1 tsp crushed allspice
juice of 2 limes
4 cod steaks
5 ml/1 tsp brown muscovado (brown) sugar
10 ml/2 tsp angostura bitters
salt
steamed okra or green beans, to serve

1 Heat the oil in a frying pan. Add the shallots and cook for 5 minutes until soft.

2 Add the garlic and chilli and cook for 2 minutes, then stir in the tomatoes, bay leaves, cayenne pepper, allspice and lime juice, with a little salt to taste.

3 Cook gently for 15 minutes, then add the cod steaks and baste with the tomato sauce. Cover and cook for 10 minutes or until the steaks are just cooked through. Remove and keep hot.

4 Stir the sugar and angostura bitters into the sauce, simmer for 2 minutes, then pour over the fish. Serve with steamed okra or green beans.

Nutritional Notes	
Energy	190 Kcals/790 kJ
Fat, total	4 g
Saturated fat	0.6 g
Cholesterol	58.5 mg

Cod, Tomato & Pepper Bake

This appetizing, potato-topped bake is filling and substantial yet relatively low in calories. It needs only a salad or lightly cooked vegetable accompaniment to make a satisfying meal.

Serves 4

INGREDIENTS
450 g/1 lb potatoes, thinly sliced
15 ml/1 tbsp olive oil
1 red onion, chopped
1 garlic clove, crushed
1 red (bell) pepper, seeded and diced
1 yellow (bell) pepper, seeded and diced
225 g/8 oz/3 cups mushrooms, sliced
400 g/14 oz and 225 g/8 oz cans chopped
    tomatoes
75 ml/5 tbsp fish or vegetable stock
75 ml/5 tbsp dry white wine
450 g/1 lb skinless, boneless cod fillet, cut
    into 2 cm/¾ in cubes
50 g/2 oz/½ cup pitted black olives, chopped
15 ml/1 tbsp chopped fresh basil
15 ml/1 tbsp chopped fresh oregano
salt and freshly ground black pepper
fresh oregano sprigs, to garnish
steamed courgettes (zucchini), to serve

1 Preheat the oven to 200°C/400°F/
Gas 6. Par-boil the potatoes in a
pan of lightly salted, boiling water
for 4 minutes. Drain thoroughly.
Set aside.

2 Heat the remaining oil in a pan,
add the onion, garlic and diced red
and yellow peppers and cook for 5
minutes, stirring occasionally.

3 Stir in the sliced mushrooms,
chopped tomatoes, stock and wine,
bring to the boil and boil rapidly for a
few minutes until the sauce has
reduced slightly.

4 Add the fish cubes and chopped
olives, basil and oregano to the tomato
mixture. Season to taste with salt and
ground black pepper.

5 Spoon into a lightly greased
ovenproof dish and arrange the potato
slices over the top, covering the fish
mixture completely.

6 Bake, uncovered, for about 45 minutes until the fish is cooked and tender and the potato topping is lightly browned. Garnish with fresh oregano sprigs and serve with steamed courgettes.

Nutritional Notes	
Energy	280 Kcals/1165 kJ
Fat, total	5.9 g
Saturated fat	0.8 g
Cholesterol	51.8 mg

Poached Salmon with Citrus Fruits

An elegant, but simple, dish with delightfully contrasting flavours.

Serves 4

INGREDIENTS

2 shallots, finely chopped
300 ml/½ pint/1¼ cups fish stock
4 salmon cutlets, about 150 g/5 oz each
1 lime
1 medium orange
1 small pink grapefruit
salt and freshly ground black pepper
steamed new potatoes, to serve (optional)

1 Place the finely chopped shallots in a wide pan with the fish stock. Simmer gently for 6–8 minutes until the stock has reduced by half and the shallots are transparent.

2 Arrange the cutlets in a single layer on the shallots, cover and simmer for 5 minutes until the fish is just cooked.

3 Remove a few strips of citrus rind and set aside. Peel and segment the fruits, collecting the juices. Add to the pan, heat and season. Garnish with rind strips and serve with potatoes, if using.

Nutritional Notes	
Energy	291 Kcals/1210 kJ
Fat, total	16.2 g
Saturated fat	3.2 g
Cholesterol	73.5 mg

Spicy Prawns with Campanelle

Serves 6

INGREDIENTS

225 g/8 oz cooked peeled tiger prawns
  (shrimp)
150 g/5 oz smoked turkey rashers (bacon)
1 shallot or small onion, finely chopped
60 ml/4 tbsp white wine
225 g/8 oz/3 cups campanelle
60 ml/4 tbsp fish stock
4 ripe tomatoes, peeled, seeded and chopped
10 g/¼ oz/2 tbsp chopped fresh parsley
salt and freshly ground black pepper

FOR THE MARINADE
1–2 garlic cloves, crushed
finely grated rind of 1 lemon
15 ml/1 tbsp lemon juice
1.5 ml/¼ tsp red chilli paste
15 ml/1 tbsp light soy sauce

1 Marinate the prawns with the marinade ingredients and seasoning for at least 1 hour.

2 Grill the turkey rashers, then cut them into 5 mm/¼ in dice.

3 Put the chopped shallot or onion and white wine into a pan, bring to the boil, cover and cook for 2–3 minutes or until the wine has reduced by half. Cook the campanelle in boiling, salted water according to the packet instructions until *al dente*. Drain thoroughly.

4 Put the prawns and marinade in a large frying pan, bring to the boil and add the turkey and stock. Heat for 1 minute, then add to the pasta with the tomatoes and parsley, toss and serve.

Nutritional Notes	
Energy	203 Kcals/844 kJ
Fat, total	1.3 g
Saturated fat	0.3 g
Cholesterol	87 mg

Chicken Baked with Butter Beans & Garlic

A whole bird is cooked slowly on a bed of garlicky vegetables.

Serves 6

INGREDIENTS
2 leeks, thickly sliced
1 small fennel bulb, roughly chopped
4 garlic cloves, peeled
2 x 400 g/14 oz cans butter (lima) beans,
    drained and rinsed
2 large handfuls fresh parsley, chopped, with
    a few sprigs reserved to garnish
300 ml/½ pint/1¼ cups dry white wine
300 ml/½ pint/1¼ cups vegetable stock
1.5 kg/3–3½ lb chicken
cooked green vegetables, to serve

1 Preheat the oven to
180°C/350°F/Gas 4. Mix the leeks,
fennel, whole garlic cloves, beans and
chopped parsley in a bowl.

2 Spread out the mixture on the
bottom of a heavy-based, flameproof
casserole large enough to hold the
chicken. Pour in the wine and stock.

3 Place the chicken on top. Bring to
the boil, cover the casserole and
transfer it to the oven. Bake for 1–1½
hours until the chicken is cooked and
so tender that it falls off the bone.
Garnish with parsley sprigs and serve
with lightly cooked green vegetables.

Nutritional Notes	
Energy	304 Kcals/1288 kJ
Fat, total	3.4 g
Saturated fat	0.8 g
Cholesterol	114 mg

Poached Chicken with Mustard Mayonnaise

This method of cooking keeps chicken succulent and tasty.

Serves 4

INGREDIENTS

1 leek, roughly chopped
1 large carrot, roughly chopped
1 celery stick, roughly chopped
1 medium onion, roughly chopped
1.5 kg/3–3½ lb chicken
15 ml/1 tbsp roughly chopped fresh parsley
10 ml/2 tsp roughly chopped fresh thyme
6 fresh green peppercorns
60 ml/4 tbsp mustard mayonnaise (made by
    mixing reduced-calorie mayonnaise with
    Dijon mustard to taste), green salad and
    lightly cooked baby carrots, to serve

1 Place the leek, carrot, celery and onion in a large pan.

2 Place the chicken on top, cover with water and bring to the boil. Remove any scum that comes to the surface. Add the herbs and peppercorns. Simmer gently for 1 hour. Remove from the heat and cool in the broth.

3 Transfer the chicken to a board or plate and carve, removing the skin. Arrange the slices on a serving platter. Serve with mustard mayonnaise, green salad and lightly cooked baby carrots.

Nutritional Notes	
Energy	153 Kcals/636 kJ
Fat, total	5 g
Saturated fat	1.4 g
Cholesterol	85 mg

Chicken with Mixed Vegetables

A stir-fry with an oriental flavour, this uses very little oil and so makes a great low–calorie main course dish.

Serves 4

INGREDIENTS

350 g/12 oz skinless chicken breast fillets
20 ml/4 tsp vegetable oil
300 ml/½ pint/1¼ cups chicken stock
75 g/3 oz/¾ cup drained, canned
   straw mushrooms
50 g/2 oz/½ cup drained, canned sliced
   bamboo shoots
50 g/2 oz/⅓ cup drained, canned water
   chestnuts, sliced
1 small carrot, sliced
50 g/2 oz/½ cup mangetouts (snowpeas)
15 ml/1 tbsp dry sherry
15 ml/1 tbsp oyster sauce
5 ml/1 tsp caster sugar
5 ml/1 tsp cornflour (cornstarch)
15 ml/1 tbsp cold water
salt and freshly ground black pepper

1 Put the chicken in a shallow bowl. Add 5 ml/1 tsp of the oil, 1.5 ml/ ¼ tsp salt and a pinch of pepper. Cover and set the chicken aside for 10 minutes in a cool place.

Nutritional Notes	
Energy	148 Kcals/615 kJ
Fat, total	5.6 g
Saturated fat	1 g
Cholesterol	61 mg

2 Bring the stock to the boil in a saucepan. Add the chicken and cook for 12 minutes or until tender. Drain and slice thickly, reserving 75 ml/ 5 tbsp of the stock.

3 Heat the remaining oil in a non-stick frying pan or wok, add all the vegetables and stir-fry for 2 minutes. Stir in the sherry, oyster sauce, caster sugar and reserved stock. Add the chicken to the pan and cook for 2 minutes more.

4 Mix the cornflour to a paste with the water. Add the mixture to the pan and cook, stirring, until the sauce thickens slightly. Season to taste with salt and pepper and serve immediately.

VARIATION: Try courgettes, broccoli and beansprouts, if you like.

31

Turkey Picadillo

Using minced turkey rather than beef for this Mexican–style dish makes it much lower in calories.

Serves 4

INGREDIENTS
15 ml/1 tbsp sunflower oil
1 onion, chopped
250 g/9 oz minced (ground) turkey
1–2 garlic cloves, crushed
1 fresh green chilli, seeded and finely chopped
6 tomatoes, peeled and chopped
15 ml/1 tbsp tomato purée (paste) or sun-dried tomato purée (paste)
2.5 ml/½ tsp ground cumin
1 yellow or orange (bell) pepper, chopped
25 g/1 oz/⅙ cup raisins
25 g/1 oz/¼ cup flaked almonds, toasted (optional)
45 ml/3 tbsp chopped fresh coriander (cilantro)
150 ml/¼ pint/⅔ cup plain low-fat yogurt
2–3 spring onions (scallions), finely chopped
4 small soft tortillas
salt and freshly ground black pepper
shredded lettuce, to serve

1 Heat the oil in a large frying pan and add the onion. Cook gently until soft. Stir in the minced turkey and garlic and cook gently for 5 minutes.

> VARIATION: Turkey Picadillo and the topping can also be used with baked jacket potatoes; adjust your calorie count accordingly.

2 Stir in the green chilli, chopped tomatoes, tomato purée, cumin, yellow or orange pepper and raisins. Cover and cook over a gentle heat for 15 minutes, stirring occasionally and adding a little water if necessary.

3 Stir in the toasted almonds, if using, with about two-thirds of the coriander. Add salt and pepper to taste.

4 Tip the low-fat yogurt into a bowl. Stir in the remaining coriander and the chopped spring onions. Heat the tortillas in a dry frying pan, without oil, for 15–20 seconds.

5 Place some shredded lettuce and turkey mixture on each tortilla, roll up like a pancake and transfer to a plate. Top with a generous spoonful of the yogurt and coriander mixture and serve immediately.

Nutritional Notes	
Energy	295 Kcals/1225 kJ
Fat, total	8.6 g
Saturated fat	0.9 g
Cholesterol	45.3 mg

Chinese Pork

It is worth allowing plenty of time for marinating this lean pork fillet, which is then roasted to produce a truly mouthwatering result. Steamed vegetables would complement the richness of the pork perfectly.

Serves 6

INGREDIENTS
900 g/2 lb pork fillet, trimmed
15 ml/1 tbsp clear honey
45 ml/3 tbsp rice wine or medium-dry sherry
spring onion (scallion) curls, to garnish

FOR THE MARINADE
150 ml/¼ pint/⅔ cup dark soy sauce
90 ml/6 tbsp rice wine or medium-dry sherry
150 ml/¼ pint/⅔ cup well-flavoured chicken stock
15 ml/1 tbsp soft brown sugar
1 cm/½ in piece fresh root ginger, peeled and finely sliced
40 ml/2½ tbsp chopped onion

1 To make the marinade, place all the ingredients in a pan and stir over a medium heat until the mixture boils. Lower the heat and simmer gently for 15 minutes, stirring from time to time. Leave to cool.

Nutritional Notes	
Energy	206 Kcals/856 kJ
Fat, total	6 g
Saturated fat	2.1 g
Cholesterol	94.5 mg

2 Put the pork fillet in a shallow dish that is large enough to hold it in a single layer. Pour over 250 ml/8 fl oz/1 cup of the marinade, cover and chill for at least 8 hours, turning the meat several times.

3 Preheat the oven to 200°C/400°F/Gas 6. Drain the pork, reserving the marinade in the dish. Place the meat on a rack over a roasting tin and pour water into the tin to a depth of 1 cm/½ in. Place the tin in the oven and roast for 20 minutes.

4 Stir the honey and rice wine or sherry into the marinade. Remove the meat from the oven and place in the marinade, turning to coat.

5 Put the meat back on the rack and roast for 20–30 minutes more or until cooked. Serve hot or cold, in slices, garnished with spring onion curls

COOK'S TIP: To make spring onion curls, cut spring onions down to 7.5 cm/3 in lengths, then cut lengthways, leaving the root end intact. Place in iced water and chill until curled.

Skewered Lamb with Red Onion Salsa

A low-calorie dish that is bursting with taste sensations, both from the spicy marinade coating the lamb and the fresh vegetables and herbs of the salsa.

Serves 2

INGREDIENTS
225 g/8 oz lean lamb, cubed
2.5 ml/½ tsp ground cumin
5 ml/1 tsp ground paprika
15 ml/1 tbsp olive oil
salt and freshly ground black pepper

FOR THE SALSA
1 red onion, very thinly sliced
1 large tomato, seeded and chopped
15 ml/1 tbsp red wine vinegar
3–4 fresh basil or mint leaves, roughly torn
small mint leaves, to garnish

1 Place the lamb in a bowl with the cumin, paprika, oil and plenty of salt and pepper. Toss well until the lamb is coated with spices.

2 Cover the bowl with clear film (plastic wrap) and leave in a cool place for several hours, or in the fridge overnight, to marinade the lamb.

VARIATION: For an alternative to the red onion salsa, stir chopped fresh mint or basil and a little lemon juice into a small pot of low-fat Greek-style yogurt. Adjust your calorie count accordingly.

3 Spear the lamb cubes on to four small skewers – if using wooden skewers, soak them first in cold water for at least 30 minutes to prevent them burning under the grill (broiler).

4 To make the salsa, put the onion, tomato, vinegar and basil or mint leaves in a small bowl and stir together until thoroughly blended. Season to taste with salt, garnish with mint, then set aside while you cook the lamb.

5 Cook the lamb over hot coals or under a preheated grill for about 5–10 minutes, turning the skewers frequently, until the lamb is well browned but still slightly pink in the centre. Serve hot, with the salsa.

Nutritional Notes	
Energy	132 Kcals/549 kJ
Fat, total	7.6 g
Saturated fat	2.5 g
Cholesterol	41.6 mg

Beef Strips with Orange & Ginger

This delicious, lean beef dish is quickly prepared by stir-frying, one of the best methods of low-calorie cooking.

Serves 4

INGREDIENTS
450 g/1 lb lean beef rump, fillet or sirloin,
    cut into thin strips
finely grated rind and juice of 1 orange
15 ml/1 tbsp light soy sauce
5 ml/1 tsp cornflour (cornstarch)
2.5 cm/1 in piece fresh root ginger, peeled
    and finely chopped
10 ml/2 tsp sesame oil
1 large carrot, cut into thin strips
2 spring onions (scallions), thinly sliced
cooked rice noodles, to serve

3 Heat the oil in a wok or large frying pan and add the beef. Stir-fry for 1 minute until lightly coloured, then add the carrot and stir-fry for a further 2–3 minutes.

1 Place the beef strips in a bowl and sprinkle over the orange rind and juice. If possible, leave to marinate for at least 30 minutes.

2 Drain the liquid from the meat and set aside, then mix the marinade with the soy sauce, cornflour and ginger.

4 Stir in the spring onions and reserved liquid, then cook, stirring, until boiling and thickened. Serve hot with rice noodles.

VARIATION: Lean pork tenderloin or fillet could be used instead of beef. Adjust your calorie count accordingly.

Nutritional Notes	
Energy	175 Kcals/730 kJ
Fat, total	6.81 g
Saturated fat	2.31 g
Cholesterol	66.37 mg

COOK'S TIP: It is important to choose lean, tender meat for stir-fries like this, as it is cooked in the minimum of time.

Jamaican Black Bean Pot

Molasses imparts a rich, treacly flavour to the spicy sauce, which incorporates a stunning mix of black beans, vibrant red and yellow (bell) peppers and orange butternut squash.

Serves 4

INGREDIENTS
225 g/8 oz/1¼ cups dried black beans
1 bay leaf
15 ml/1 tbsp vegetable oil
1 large onion, chopped
1 garlic clove, chopped
5 ml/1 tsp English mustard powder
15 ml/1 tbsp blackstrap molasses
30 ml/2 tbsp soft dark brown sugar
5 ml/1 tsp dried thyme
2.5 ml/½ tsp dried chilli flakes
5 ml/1 tsp vegetable bouillon powder
1 red (bell) pepper, seeded and diced
1 yellow (bell) pepper, seeded and diced
450 g/1 lb/5¼ cups butternut squash or
    pumpkin, seeded and cut into 1 cm/½ in
    dice
salt and freshly ground black pepper
fresh thyme sprigs, to garnish
boiled rice, to serve

1 Soak the beans overnight in plenty of water, then drain and rinse well. Place in a large pan, cover with fresh water and add the bay leaf.

Nutritional Notes	
Energy	283 Kcals/1176 kJ
Fat, total	4.1 g
Saturated fat	0.7 g
Cholesterol	0 mg

2 Bring to the boil, then boil rapidly for 10 minutes. Reduce the heat, cover, and simmer for 30 minutes until tender. Drain, reserving the cooking water. Preheat the oven to 180°C/350°F/Gas 4.

3 Heat the oil in a frying pan and sauté the onion and garlic for about 5 minutes until softened, stirring occasionally. Add the mustard powder, molasses, sugar, dried thyme and chilli and cook for 1 minute, stirring. Stir in the black beans, then spoon the mixture into a flameproof casserole.

4 Add enough water to the reserved bean cooking liquid to make 400 ml/14 fl oz/1⅔ cups, then mix in the bouillon powder and pour into the casserole. Stir into the beans, then bake in the oven for 25 minutes.

5 Add the peppers and squash or pumpkin and mix well. Cover, then bake for 45 minutes more until the vegetables are tender. Serve garnished with fresh thyme and accompanied by boiled rice.

Braised Barley & Vegetables

One of the oldest of cultivated cereals, pot barley has a nutty flavour and slightly chewy texture. It makes a warming and filling dish when combined with root vegetables.

Serves 4

INGREDIENTS
200 g/7 oz/1 cup pearl or pot barley
15 ml/1 tbsp sunflower oil
1 large onion, chopped
2 celery sticks, sliced
2 carrots, sliced thickly
225 g/8 oz swede (rutabaga) or turnip, cut
    into 2 cm/¾ in cubes
225 g/8 oz potatoes, cut into 2 cm/¾ in cubes
475 ml/16 fl oz/2 cups vegetable stock
salt and freshly ground black pepper
celery leaves, to garnish

1 Put the barley in a measuring jug and add water to reach the 600 ml/1 pint/2½ cup mark. Leave to soak in a cool place for at least 4 hours or, preferably, overnight.

2 Heat the oil in a large pan and fry the onion for 5 minutes. Add the celery and carrots and cook for 3–4 minutes or until the onion is starting to brown.

3 Add the barley and its soaking liquid to the pan. Then add the swede or turnip, potatoes and stock. Season with salt and pepper. Bring to the boil, reduce the heat and cover the pan.

4 Simmer for 40 minutes or until most of the stock has been absorbed and the barley is tender. Stir occasionally towards the end of cooking to prevent the barley from sticking to the base of the pan. Serve garnished with celery leaves.

Nutritional Notes	
Energy	297 Kcals/1235 kJ
Fat, total	4.2 g
Saturated fat	0.4 g
Cholesterol	0 mg

Balti Potatoes with Aubergines

A heavenly mixture of Balti spices enhances this low–calorie dish.

Serves 4

INGREDIENTS
10–12 baby potatoes
6 small aubergines (eggplant)
1 medium red (bell) pepper
15 ml/1 tbsp corn oil
2 medium onions, sliced
4–6 curry leaves
2.5 ml/½ tsp onion seeds
5 ml/1 tsp crushed coriander seeds
2.5 ml/½ tsp cumin seeds
5 ml/1 tsp finely chopped fresh root ginger
5 ml/1 tsp crushed garlic
5 ml/1 tsp crushed dried red chillies
15 ml/1 tbsp chopped fresh fenugreek
5 ml/1 tsp chopped fresh coriander (cilantro),
    plus whole leaves to garnish
15 ml/1 tbsp plain low-fat yogurt

1 Cook the unpeeled potatoes in boiling water until just soft. Set aside. Cut the aubergines into quarters. Cut the red pepper in half, discard the seeds, then slice the flesh into strips.

2 Heat the oil in a non–stick wok and fry the onions, curry leaves, onion seeds, crushed coriander seeds and cumin seeds for 5 minutes or until the onions are a soft golden brown.

3 Add the ginger, garlic, chillies and fenugreek, followed by the pepper, aubergines and potatoes. Stir everything together and cover with a lid. Lower the heat and cook for 5–7 minutes.

4 Remove the lid, add the chopped coriander followed by the yogurt, and stir well. Serve garnished with whole coriander leaves.

Nutritional Notes	
Energy	150 Kcals/624 kJ
Fat, total	3.6 g
Saturated fat	0.6 g
Cholesterol	0.2 mg

COOK'S TIP: To prevent curdling, it is always best to whisk yogurt before adding it to a hot dish.

Red Cabbage & Apple Casserole

The brilliant colour and pungent flavour make this an excellent winter dish.

Serves 6

INGREDIENTS
3 onions, chopped
2 fennel bulbs, roughly chopped
675 g/1½ lb red cabbage, shredded
30 ml/2 tbsp caraway seeds
3 tart eating apples or 1 large cooking apple
300 ml/½ pint/1¼ cups plain low-fat yogurt
15 ml/1 tbsp creamed horseradish sauce
salt and freshly ground black pepper

Nutritional Notes	
Energy	98 Kcals/407 kJ
Fat, total	1.2 g
Saturated fat	0.3 g
Cholesterol	18 mg

1 Preheat the oven to 150°C/300°F/ Gas 2. Mix the onions, fennel, cabbage and caraway seeds in a bowl. Peel and chop the apples, then stir them into the cabbage mixture.

2 Transfer to a casserole. Mix the yogurt with the creamed horseradish sauce and stir into the casserole.

3 Season with salt and pepper and cover tightly. Bake for 1½ hours, stirring once or twice. Serve hot.

COOK'S TIP: This casserole can be served with plain boiled rice. Include this in your calorie count.

Vegetable Casserole

Serves 4

INGREDIENTS
15 ml/1 tbsp olive oil
675 g/1½ lb frozen broad (fava) beans
4 turnips, sliced
4 leeks, sliced
1 red (bell) pepper, seeded and sliced
200 g/7 oz fresh spinach leaves or 115 g/4 oz frozen spinach
2 x 400 g/14 oz cans artichoke hearts, drained
30 ml/2 tbsp pumpkin seeds
soy sauce
salt and freshly ground black pepper
rice, baked jacket potatoes or wholemeal (whole-wheat) bread, to serve (optional)

1 Preheat the oven to 180°C/350°F/ Gas 4. Brush a casserole with the oil.

2 Cook the broad beans in a saucepan of boiling, lightly salted water for about 10 minutes. Drain and place with the next five ingredients in the casserole. Cover the casserole and bake in the oven for 30–40 minutes or until the turnips are soft.

3 Stir in the pumpkin seeds and soy sauce to taste. Season with pepper. Serve alone or with rice, baked jacket potatoes or bread, if you prefer.

Nutritional Notes	
Energy	258 Kcals/1074 kJ
Fat, total	9.0 g
Saturated fat	1.3 g
Cholesterol	0 mg

Fettuccine with Broccoli & Garlic

Just add a mixed salad to make this a complete and delicious main course.

Serves 4

INGREDIENTS
3–4 garlic cloves, crushed
350 g/12 oz/3 cups broccoli florets
150 ml/¼ pint/⅔ cup vegetable stock
60 ml/4 tbsp white wine
30 ml/2 tbsp chopped fresh basil
60 ml/4 tbsp grated Parmesan cheese
350 g/12 oz/3 cups fettuccine or tagliatelle
salt and freshly ground black pepper
fresh basil leaves, to garnish
mixed leaf salad, to serve

1 Cook the garlic and broccoli in the stock for 5 minutes until tender. Mash roughly with a fork or potato masher. Add the wine, basil and Parmesan cheese. Season to taste.

2 Cook the fettuccine or tagliatelle in a large pan of boiling, salted water according to the packet instructions until *al dente*. Drain thoroughly.

3 Return the pasta to the pan with half the broccoli sauce, toss to coat, then transfer to serving plates. Top with the remaining broccoli sauce, garnish with basil leaves and serve with salad.

Nutritional Notes	
Energy	411 Kcals/1709 kJ
Fat, total	7.3 g
Saturated fat	3.5 g
Cholesterol	15 mg

Risotto Primavera

A substantial one-pot vegetarian main dish that is low in calories.

Serves 4

INGREDIENTS

10 ml/2 tsp olive oil
1 medium onion, sliced
250 g/9 oz/1¼ cups short grain rice
2.5 ml/½ tsp ground turmeric
500 ml/1 pint/2½ cups vegetable stock
250 g/9 oz mixed spring vegetables, left
  whole if small
45 ml/3 tbsp chopped fresh parsley
salt and freshly ground black pepper
30 ml/2 tbsp grated Parmesan cheese
  (optional), to serve

1 Heat the oil in a non-stick pan and fry the onion until golden. Stir in the rice and cook for 1–2 minutes.

2 Add the turmeric, vegetable stock and seasoning. Bring to the boil, then add the vegetables.

3 Return to the boil, cover the pan and cook gently, stirring occasionally, for 20 minutes or until the rice is tender and most of the liquid has been absorbed. Add more stock if necessary.

4 Stir in the parsley and adjust the seasoning to taste. Serve hot, lightly sprinkled with Parmesan, if using.

Nutritional Notes	
Energy	102 Kcals/424 kJ
Fat, total	0.4 g
Saturated fat	0.04 g
Cholesterol	0 mg

Rice Noodles with Vegetable Chilli Sauce

The vegetables here are red pepper, carrots, baby sweetcorn, bamboo shoots and kidney beans, gently simmered together in a spicy sauce.

Serves 4

INGREDIENTS
15 ml/1 tbsp sunflower oil
1 onion, chopped
2 garlic cloves, crushed
1 fresh red chilli, seeded and finely chopped
1 red (bell) pepper, seeded and diced
1 carrot, finely chopped
175 g/6 oz/1 cup baby sweetcorn, halved
225 g/8 oz can sliced bamboo shoots, rinsed and drained
200 g/7 oz can red kidney beans, rinsed and drained
300 ml/½ pint/1¼ cups passata or sieved tomatoes
15 ml/1 tbsp soy sauce
5 ml/1 tsp ground coriander
175 g/6 oz rice noodles
30 ml/2 tbsp chopped fresh coriander (cilantro) or parsley
salt and freshly ground black pepper
fresh parsley sprigs, to garnish

1 Heat the oil, add the onion, garlic, chilli and red pepper and cook for 5 minutes, stirring. Stir in the carrot, sweetcorn, bamboo shoots, kidney beans, passata or sieved tomatoes, soy sauce and ground coriander.

2 Bring to the boil, then cover, reduce the heat and simmer gently for 30 minutes, or until the vegetables are tender, stirring occasionally. Season with salt and pepper to taste.

3 Meanwhile, place the noodles in a bowl and cover with boiling water. Stir with a fork and leave to stand for 3–4 minutes or according to the packet instructions. Rinse with boiling water and drain thoroughly.

Nutritional Notes	
Energy	274 Kcals/1140 kJ
Fat, total	3.8 g
Saturated fat	0.4 g
Cholesterol	0 mg

COOK'S TIP: After handling chillies, wash your hands, as the oils can burn your eyes, if touched.

4 Stir the fresh coriander or parsley into the sauce. Spoon the noodles on to warmed serving plates and top with the sauce. Garnish with parsley sprigs and serve.

Poached Pears in Maple-yogurt Sauce

An elegant dessert, ideal for low-calorie entertaining, that is easier to make than it looks – poach the pears in advance, and have the cooled syrup ready to spoon on to the plates just before serving.

Serves 6

INGREDIENTS
6 firm dessert pears
15 ml/1 tbsp lemon juice
250 ml/8 fl oz/1 cup sweet white wine or cider
thinly pared rind of 1 lemon
1 cinnamon stick
30 ml/2 tbsp maple syrup
2.5 ml/½ tsp arrowroot
150 g/5 oz/⅔ cup low-fat Greek-style
(strained, low-fat) yogurt

1 Thinly peel the pears, leaving them whole and with stalks intact. Brush them with lemon juice to prevent them from browning. Scoop out the core from the base of each pear.

2 Place the pears in a wide, heavy-based pan and pour over the wine or cider, with enough cold water almost to cover the pears.

3 Add the lemon rind and cinnamon stick, then bring to the boil. Reduce the heat, cover the pan and simmer the pears gently for 30–40 minutes or until just tender. Turn the pears occasionally so that they cook evenly. Lift out the pears carefully, draining them well.

4 Bring the liquid to the boil and boil, uncovered, to reduce to about 120 ml/4 fl oz/½ cup. Strain and add the maple syrup. Blend a little of the liquid with the arrowroot. Return to the pan and cook, stirring, until thick and clear. Cool.

5 Slice each pear about three-quarters of the way through, leaving the slices attached at the stem end. Fan out each pear on a serving plate.

6 Stir 30 ml/2 tbsp of the cooled pear syrup into the yogurt and spoon it around the fanned pears. Serve immediately.

Nutritional Notes	
Energy	173 Kcals/719 kJ
Fat, total	0.31 g
Saturated fat	0.2 g
Cholesterol	1.5 mg

Cinnamon & Apricot Soufflés

Don't expect this to be difficult simply because it is a soufflé – it really could not be easier and, best of all, it is very low in calories.

Serves 4

INGREDIENTS
a little low-fat spread, for greasing
a little plain (all-purpose) flour, for dusting
3 eggs
115 g/4 oz/scant ½ cup apricot fruit spread
finely grated rind of ½ lemon
5 ml/1 tsp ground cinnamon,
   plus extra to decorate

2 Separate the eggs and place the yolks in a bowl with the apricot fruit spread, lemon rind and cinnamon. Whisk hard until the mixture is thick and pale in colour.

3 Place the egg whites in a clean bowl and whisk them until they are stiff enough to hold soft peaks.

1 Preheat the oven to 190°C/375°F/ Gas 5. Grease four individual soufflé dishes and dust them with flour.

COOK'S TIP: Puréed fresh or well-drained canned fruit can be used instead of the apricot spread, but make sure the mixture is not too wet or the soufflé will not rise properly. Adjust your calorie count accordingly.

4 Using a metal spoon or spatula, fold the beaten egg whites evenly into the yolk mixture.

5 Divide the soufflé mixture among the prepared dishes and bake for 10–15 minutes until well-risen and golden brown. Serve the soufflés immediately, dusted with a little extra ground cinnamon.

Nutritional Notes	
Energy	98 Kcals/407 kJ
Fat, total	4.6 g
Saturated fat	1.3 g
Cholesterol	164.5 mg

Strawberry Gâteau

It is hard to believe that this delicious gâteau is low in calories, but it is true, so enjoy! Ring the changes with other soft fruits, if you like.

Serves 6

INGREDIENTS
2 eggs
75 g/3 oz/6 tbsp caster (superfine) sugar
grated rind of ½ orange
50 g/2 oz/½ cup plain (all-purpose) flour
strawberry leaves, to decorate (optional)
icing sugar, for dusting

FOR THE FILLING
275 g/10 oz/1¼ cups low-fat soft cheese
grated rind of ½ orange
30 ml/2 tbsp caster (superfine) sugar
60 ml/4 tbsp low-fat fromage frais
225 g/8 oz/2 cups strawberries, halved
25 g/1 oz/¼ cup chopped almonds, toasted

1 Preheat the oven to 190°C/375°F/Gas 5. Grease a 30 x 20 cm/12 x 8 in Swiss roll tin and line with non-stick baking paper.

2 In a bowl, whisk the eggs, sugar and orange rind together until thick and mousse-like.

3 Fold in the flour. Turn into the prepared tin. Bake for 15–20 minutes or until the cake springs back when lightly pressed. Turn out on to a wire rack, remove the paper and leave to cool.

4 Meanwhile, to make the filling, mix the soft cheese with the orange rind, sugar and fromage frais. Divide between two bowls. Chop half the strawberry halves and add to one bowl of filling.

5 Cut the sponge widthways into three equal pieces and sandwich them together with the strawberry filling. Spread two-thirds of the plain filling over the sides of the cake and press on the toasted almonds.

Nutritional Notes	
Energy	151 Kcals/628 kJ
Fat, total	4.5 g
Saturated fat	0.8 g
Cholesterol	73.7 mg

6 Spread the rest of the filling over the top of the cake and decorate with the remaining strawberry halves, and strawberry leaves, if liked. Dust with icing sugar and serve.

Mango & Amaretti Strudel

Fresh mango and crushed amaretti wrapped in wafer-thin filo pastry make a special treat that is high in scrumptiousness but low in calories.

Serves 4

INGREDIENTS
1 large mango
grated rind of 1 lemon
2 amaretti biscuits
25 g/1 oz/2 tbsp demerara sugar
15 g/½ oz/3 tbsp wholemeal (whole-wheat) breadcrumbs
2 sheets filo pastry, each 48 x 28 cm/19 x 11 in, defrosted if frozen
10 g/½ tbsp low-fat soft margarine, melted
10 g/¼ oz/1 tbsp chopped almonds
icing (confectioner's) sugar, for dusting

1 Preheat the oven to 190°C/375°FGas 5. Lightly grease a large baking sheet. Cut the mango on each side of the stone. Peel, and cut the flesh into cubes, then place them in a bowl and sprinkle with the grated lemon rind.

2 Crush the amaretti biscuits and mix them with the demerara sugar and the wholemeal breadcrumbs.

3 Lay one sheet of filo on a flat surface and brush with a quarter of the melted margarine. Top with the second sheet, brush with one-third of the remaining margarine, then fold both sheets over to make a rectangle measuring 28 x 24 cm/11 x 9½ in. Brush with half the remaining margarine.

4 Sprinkle the filo with the amaretti mixture, leaving a 5 cm/2 in border on each long side. Arrange the mango cubes over the top.

5 Roll up the filo from one of the long sides. Lift the strudel on to the baking sheet with the join underneath. Brush with the remaining margarine and sprinkle with almonds.

Nutritional Notes	
Energy	188 Kcals/781 kJ
Fat, total	3.8 g
Saturated fat	0.6 g
Cholesterol	1.7 mg

6 Bake for 20–25 minutes until golden brown, then transfer to a board. Dust with the icing sugar, slice diagonally and serve warm.

COOK'S TIP: During preparation, cover unused filo with a damp dish towel to prevent it from drying.

Baked Blackberry Cheesecake

This light, low-calorie cheesecake is best made with wild blackberries, if available, though cultivated ones will produce a good result.

Serves 5

INGREDIENTS

175 g/6 oz/¾ cup cottage cheese
150 g/5 oz/⅔ cup plain low-fat yogurt
15 ml/1 tbsp plain wholemeal (whole-wheat) flour
25 g/1 oz/2 tbsp golden caster (superfine) sugar
1 egg
1 egg white
finely grated rind and juice of ½ lemon
200 g/7 oz/2 cups fresh or frozen blackberries, thawed

1 Preheat the oven to 180°C/350°F/Gas 4. Lightly grease and base-line an 18 cm/7 in sandwich tin (pan).

3 Place the cottage cheese in a bowl, add the low-fat yogurt, wholemeal flour, caster sugar, egg and egg white, and mix thoroughly. Add the lemon rind and juice and blackberries, reserving a few for decoration.

4 Tip the cheesecake mixture into the prepared sandwich tin and bake for 30–35 minutes, or until just set. Turn off the oven and leave for a further 30 minutes.

2 Place the cottage cheese in a food processor and process until smooth. Alternatively, rub it through a sieve to achieve a smooth texture.

5 Run a knife around the edge of the cheesecake to loosen it from the tin, and carefully turn it out. Remove the lining paper.

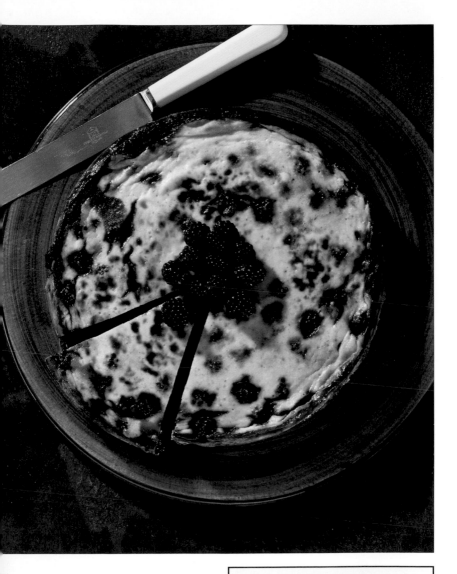

6 Place the cheesecake on a warm serving plate. Decorate with the reserved blackberries and serve warm.

Nutritional Notes	
Energy	100 Kcals/416 kJ
Fat, total	2.11 g
Saturated fat	0.8 g
Cholesterol	46.8 mg

Apple & Banana Crumble

A fabulous, low-calorie version of an old favourite, with a natural sweetness.

Serves 6

INGREDIENTS

2 large cooking apples, cored and chopped
2 large bananas, peeled and sliced
60 ml/4 tbsp water
25 g/1 oz/2 tbsp low-fat spread
30–45 ml/2–3 tbsp pear and apple spread
25 g/1 oz/¼ cup wholemeal (whole-wheat) flour
75 g/3 oz/¾ cup porridge oats
15 ml/1 tbsp sunflower seeds
low-fat yogurt, to serve (optional)

1 Preheat the oven to 180°C/350°F/ Gas 4. Mix the apples, bananas and water in a pan and cook until soft and pulpy.

2 Melt the low-fat spread with the pear and apple spread in a separate pan. Stir in the flour, oats and sunflower seeds, and mix well.

3 Transfer the apple and banana mixture to an 18 cm/7 in baking dish and spread the oat crumble over the top. Bake for about 20 minutes or until the topping is golden brown. Serve warm or at room temperature, alone or with low-fat yogurt, if liked.

Nutritional Notes	
Energy	176 Kcals/733 kJ
Fat, total	4.3 g
Saturated fat	0.8 g
Cholesterol	0.3 mg

Banana & Pineapple Ice Cream

Half the cream is substituted with low-calorie yogurt for a superb ice cream.

Serves 4

INGREDIENTS
1 banana
150 g/5 oz fresh pineapple
150 ml/¼ pint/⅔ cup plain low-fat yogurt
150 ml/¼ pint/⅔ cup whipping cream, lightly
   whipped
fresh mint sprig, to decorate

1 Purée the banana and pineapple in a blender or food processor. Tip the purée into a large bowl and stir in the yogurt. Fold in the cream.

COOK'S TIP: Drained canned pineapple in fruit juice can be substituted for the fresh pineapple.

2 Churn the mixture in an ice-cream maker. Alternatively, place it in a suitable container for freezing. Freeze for about 2 hours until ice crystals form around the edges. Process or beat the mixture until it is smooth, then return it to the freezer.

3 Repeat the process once or twice, then freeze until firm. Remove from the freezer to soften slightly before serving, decorated with mint.

Nutritional Notes	
Energy	200 Kcals/832 kJ
Fat, total	15.2 g
Saturated fat	9.5 g
Cholesterol	0 mg

This edition is published by Lorenz Books, an imprint of Anness Publishing Ltd, Blaby Road, Wigston, LE18 4SE

www.lorenzbooks.com; www.annesspublishing.com

If you like the images in this book and would like to investigate using them for publishing, promotions or advertising, please visit our website www.practicalpictures.com for more information.

Publisher: Joanna Lorenz
Editor: Valerie Ferguson & Helen Sudell
Series Designer: Bobbie Colgate Stone
Designer: Andrew Heath
Production Controller: Steve Lang
Recipes contributed by: Catherine Atkinson, Michelle Berriedale-Johnson, Kathy Brown, Trish Davies, Patrizia Diemling, Christine France, Silvano Franco, Nicola Graimes, Carole Handslip, Deh-Ta Hsuing, Shedzad Husain, Lesley Mackley, Sue Maggs, Kathy Man, Sallie Morris, Maggie Pannell, Anne Sheasby, Jeni Wright.
Photography: William Adams-Lingwood, Karl Adamson, Mickie Dowie, James Duncan, Ian Garlick, Michelle Garrett, Amanda Heywood, Ferguson Hill, Janine Hosegood, David Jordan, Don Last, Patrick McLeavey, Thomas Odulate, Peter Reilly.

A CIP catalogue record for this book is available from the British Library

Cook's Notes

Bracketed terms are intended for American readers. For all recipes, quantities are given in both metric and imperial measures and, where appropriate, in standard cups and spoons. Follow one set of measures, but not a mixture, because they are not interchangeable.

Standard spoon and cup measures are level. 1 tsp = 5ml, 1 tbsp = 15ml, 1 cup = 250ml/8fl oz. Australian standard tablespoons are 20ml. Australian readers should use 3 tsp in place of 1 tbsp for measuring small quantities.

American pints are 16fl oz/2 cups. American readers should use 20fl oz/2.5 cups in place of 1 pint when measuring liquids.

Electric oven temperatures in this book are for conventional ovens. When using a fan oven, the temperature will probably need to be reduced by about 10–20°C/20–40°F. Since ovens vary, you should check with your manufacturer's instruction book for guidance.

Medium (US large) eggs are used unless otherwise stated.

Publisher's Note:

Although the advice and information in this book are believed to be accurate and true at the time of going to press, neither the authors nor the publisher can accept any legal responsibility or liability for any errors or omissions that may have been made nor for any inaccuracies nor for any loss, harm or injury that comes about from following instructions or advice in this book.

© Anness Publishing Limited 2013

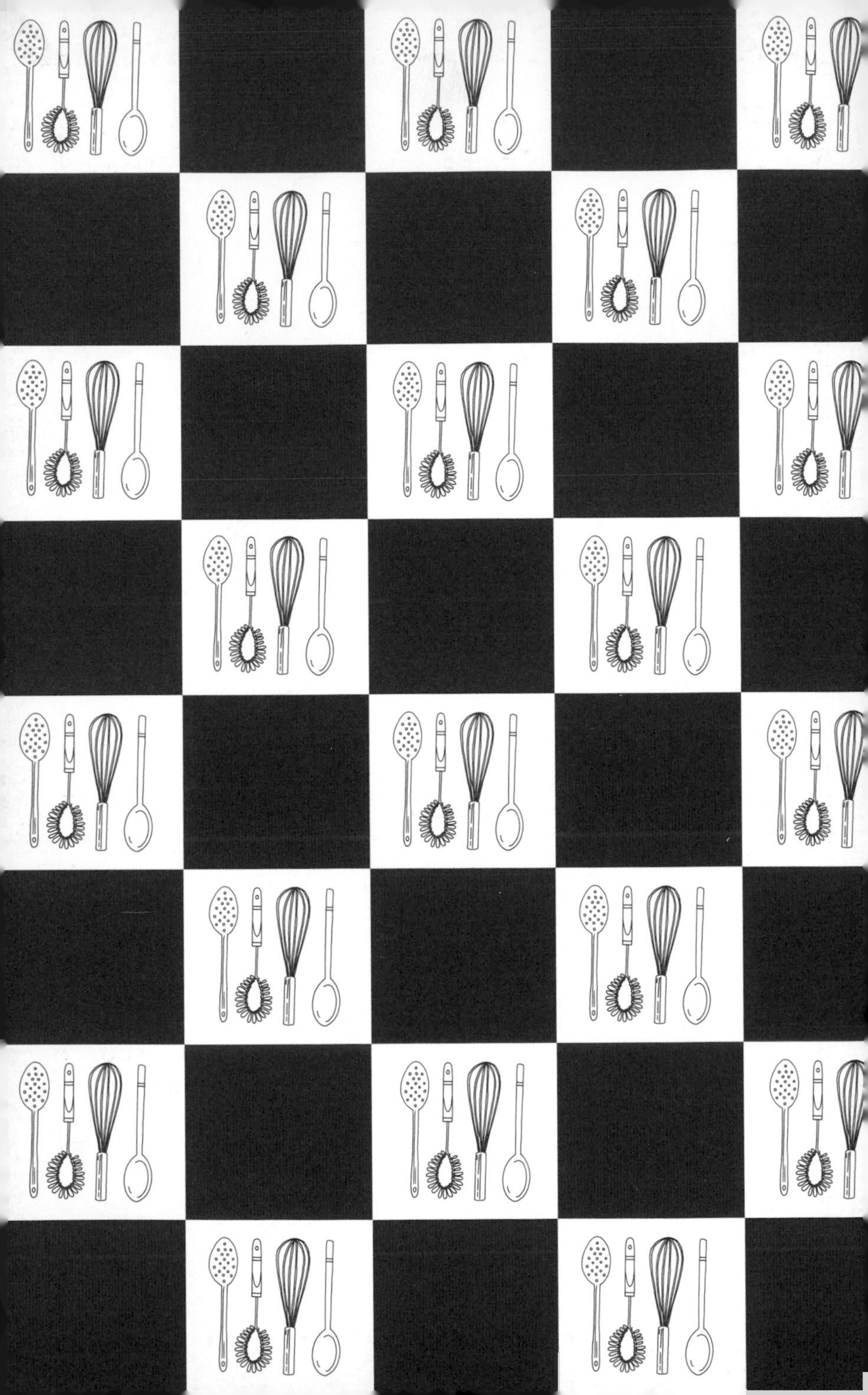